DESERT ANIMALS Searchin' for Shade

Bark Scorpion

by Meish Goldish

Consultant:

Dawn Gouge, PhD
Associate Professor and Associate Specialist, Entomology
University of Arizona
Maricopa, Arizona

BEARPORT
PUBLISHING

New York, New York

Credits

Cover, © Craig K Lorenz/GettyImages; TOC, © Ken Lucas/ardea.com; 4, © Norma Jean Gargasz/Alamy; 5, © Wechsler, Doug/Animals Animals; 7, © All Canada Photos/Alamy; 8, © Visual&Written SL/Alamy; 9, © Jack Milchanowski/Visuals Unlimited, Inc.; 10T, © All Canada Photos/Alamy; 10B, © Michael Redmer/ Visuals Unlimited/Corbis; 11TL, © Calibas/Wikipedia; 11TR, © Vitalii Hulai/Shutterstock; 11M, © Warren Photographic; 11BL, © Kletr/Shutterstock; 11BR, © Alexander Prosvirov/Shutterstock; 12, © Eric Gofreed; 13, © John Cancalosi/Alamy; 14, © Mishella/Shutterstock; 15, © Alejandro Díaz Díez; 16, © Ken Lucas/ardea. com; 17, © Robert LaMorte and Dawn Gouge; 18, © Anton Foltin/Shutterstock; 19, © Mike troll Dame; 20–21, © Wild Nature Photos/Animals Animals; 22, © Berquist, Paul & Joyce/Animals Animals; 23TL, © MISHELLA/ Shutterstock; 23TM, © Mike Troll Dame; 23TR, © Emily Tenczar; 23BL, © Ken Lucas/ardea.com; 23BM, © Alexander Prosvirov/Shutterstock; 23BR, © James C. Bartholomew/Shutterstock.

Publisher: Kenn Goin
Senior Editor: Joyce Tavolacci
Creative Director: Spencer Brinker
Design: Alix Wood
Photo Researcher: Michael Win

Library of Congress Cataloging-in-Publication Data

Goldish, Meish.
  Bark scorpion / by Meish Goldish.
      pages cm. — (Desert animals: searchin' for shade)
  Includes bibliographical references and index.
  ISBN 978-1-62724-535-7 (library binding) — ISBN 1-62724-535-9 (library binding)
  1. Centruroides—Juvenile literature. I. Title.
  QL458.72.B8G65 2015
  595.4'6—dc23
                                 2014037342

For more information, write to Bearport Publishing Company, Inc., 45 West 21st Street, Suite 3B, New York, New York 10010. Printed in the United States of America.

10 9 8 7 6 5 4 3 2 1

Contents

Behind the Bark

It is a hot, dry afternoon in the desert.

A bark scorpion rests in a tree.

It hides under the tree bark to keep out of the burning sun.

During the day, the temperature can climb to 120°F (49°C).

Yet the scorpion stays cool in the shade of the bark.

tree bark

Adult bark scorpions can be up to 3 inches (7.6 cm) long.

bark scorpion

Made for the Desert

The bark scorpion lives in the Sonoran Desert—one of the hottest deserts in North America.

The small creature is **cold-blooded**.

Its body temperature changes with the temperature of its surroundings.

To keep from overheating, the scorpion stays in a shady spot while the sun is out.

If its body becomes too hot, it will die.

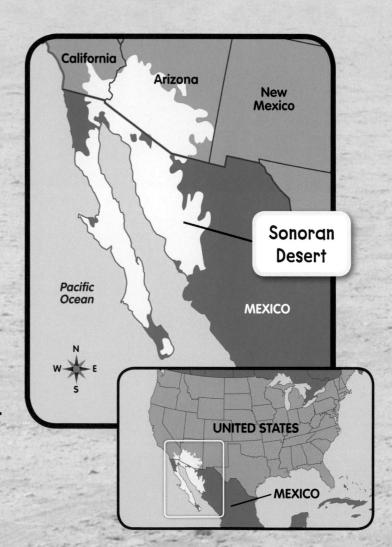

California

Arizona

New Mexico

Sonoran Desert

Pacific Ocean

MEXICO

N
W   E
S

UNITED STATES

MEXICO

Night Hunt

After the sun has set, the desert air turns cooler.

The bark scorpion climbs down from its hiding place to hunt for food.

Then it stays very still and waits for **prey** to pass by.

Even though the bark scorpion cannot see its prey in the dark, it knows when its next meal is near.

Bark scorpions are good climbers. They can climb trees, rocks, and walls.

How do you think a bark scorpion can tell when its prey is near in the dark?

Sensing Prey

A bark scorpion has tiny hairs on its legs and claw-like **pincers**.

The hairs help the scorpion sense the movements of its prey.

The hairs also tell the scorpion where its victim is.

As soon as the scorpion gets this message, it rushes over to grab its meal.

leg hairs

pincers

Bark Scorpion Foods

moth

spider

cricket

pill bug

beetle

Bark scorpions feed on insects, such as pill bugs, beetles, crickets, and moths. They also eat spiders.

How do you think a bark scorpion kills its prey?

The bark scorpion grabs its victim's legs with its pincers.

Then the scorpion curls its tail over its back and stabs the animal with it.

At the end of the scorpion's tail is a stinger.

The stinger shoots deadly poison, called **venom**, into the prey's body.

The venom causes the victim to stop moving, so the scorpion can eat it.

tail

stinger

What animals, if any, do you think attack bark scorpions?

close-up of a bark scorpion's stinger

Scorpions get most of the water they need from the food they eat.

stinger

Danger All Around

While a bark scorpion is hunting for food, larger desert animals are hunting for the scorpion.

Its enemies include owls, bats, lizards, and mice—and even other scorpions!

If it is attacked, the bark scorpion will try to run away.

If it is caught, though, it will sting its enemy to protect itself.

lizard

Owls and some other enemies will break off the scorpion's tail and stinger before eating the scorpion. That way, they don't end up swallowing the scorpion's venom.

Scorpions and People

People live in the Sonoran Desert, too.

A bark scorpion might go into a person's home to escape the desert heat.

The little creature will often hide in a dark closet, a bathroom, or in a shoe.

If it meets up with a person, it will likely use its stinger to defend itself.

The bark scorpion's sting can be very painful—and sometimes deadly.

There are about 90 kinds of scorpions in North America. Of these, the bark scorpion has the most painful and dangerous sting.

bark scorpion

When winter comes to the Sonoran Desert, it gets very cold.

Bark scorpions **hibernate** to escape the near-freezing temperatures.

They find shelter in holes in the ground or under rocks.

They go without food until spring.

At that time, it is warm enough for them to come out and hunt again.

Bark scorpions hibernate in groups of about 40.

Babies on Board

Spring is the time when male and female bark scorpions **mate**.

Then, during summer, the female gives birth to about 30 babies.

The mother scorpion pulls her babies onto her back.

She carries them around for up to three weeks.

After that, the young scorpions are grown up enough to make their own lives in the desert!

baby bark scorpions

Bark scorpions live for about six years.

Science Lab

Be a Bark Scorpion Scientist

Imagine you are a scientist who studies bark scorpions. Write a report about the scorpion's activities.

Begin your report by describing what the bark scorpion does during the day. Then describe what it does at night. Use the information in this book to help you.

Draw pictures to include in your report.

When you are finished, share your report with friends and family.

Here are some words you can use when writing about a bark scorpion's activities.

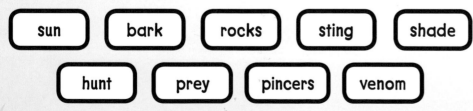

sun · bark · rocks · sting · shade

hunt · prey · pincers · venom

Read the questions below and think about the answers.

You can include some of the information from your answers in your report.

- *Where does a bark scorpion go during the day?*

- *Why does a bark scorpion come out only at night?*

- *How does a bark scorpion catch its prey?*

- *What happens if an enemy tries to catch a bark scorpion?*

cold-blooded (KOHLD-*bluhd*-id) having a body temperature that changes with the temperature of the surroundings

hibernate (HYE-bur-nayt) to spend winter in an inactive state

mate (MAYT) to come together in order to have young

pincers (PIN-surz) the claw-like body parts that a scorpion uses for grabbing and pulling

prey (PRAY) an animal that is hunted and eaten by another animal

venom (VEN-uhm) poison that some animals inject into other animals through a sting or bite

Index

Read More

Ganeri, Anita. *Scorpion (A Day in the Life: Desert Animals).* Chicago: Heinemann (2011).

Lunis, Natalie. *Stinging Scorpions (No Backbone!).* New York: Bearport (2009).

Pringle, Lawrence. *Scorpions! Strange and Wonderful.* Honesdale, PA: Boyds Mills Press (2013).

Learn More Online

To learn more about bark scorpions, visit **www.bearportpublishing.com/DesertAnimals**

About the Author

Meish Goldish has written more than 200 books for children. His book *Surf Dog Miracles* was a Children's Choices Selection in 2014. He lives in Brooklyn, New York, about 2,500 miles (4,023 km) from the Sonoran Desert.